THE PAGE OF CUPS

(SHUT UP AND DRINK!!)

A Meadmaker's Guide

Timothy Belcher
Edited and annoyed into existence
by K. J. Joyner[1]

---

[1] What this means is K. J. wrote most of the book.

Page of Cups, The
Belcher, Timothy; Joyner, K. J.
Second edition
ISBN: 978-1-944322-08-3 (pbk)

Published by the Writers of the Apocalypse
www.apocalypsewriters.com

WRITERS OF THE
APOCALYPSE

1117 N Carbon ST PMB 208
Marion, IL 62959

All rights reserved

Photos, recipe bee and cover art by Katrina Joyner. All other buzzing bees by Rebecca Pinder.
Cover chalice is an illustration from a collection of the Bros. Grimm translated from the German by Lucy Crane, 1882. All other images by public domain or photographed by K. J. Joyner.

(License notes) All Rights Reserved. No part of this book may be reproduced or transmitted in any form or by any means, graphic, electronic, or mechanical, including photocopying, recording, taping, or by any information storage retrieval system, without the written permission of the publisher.

Legal notes: The methods in this book, when used properly, may produce alcoholic beverages which should be consumed only by those of legal age. Before brewing, make sure to check the laws of your state and follow state and federal guidelines. The author assumes no responsibility for the misuse of the information provided within this document. As always brew and drink responsibly.

Contents

OPENING NOTE 11

INTRODUCTION 16

THE OBLIGATORY HISTORY AND TRADITION OF MEAD CHAPTER 18

KANU Y MED (SONG OF MEAD) 31
   Norse Riddle 33

THE TYPES OF MEAD 34

WHAT KINDS OF HONEY? 37
   Incredibly nifty list of ways to buy lots and lots of honey: 39

EQUIPMENT FOR BREWING. 41

PREPARING THE SACRED NECTAR OF THE GODS 46
   Step One: Preparation for the brewing session 46
   Step Two: How to Prepare the Must 47
   Step three: Adding Acid 51
   Step four: Yeasts 53
   Step Five: Fermentation 57
   Racking the mead 59
   Step Six: Stopping fermentation (the horror) 61
   Step Seven: Bottling Your Brew 62

The Handy Dandy List to Acquiring Copious Amounts of Bottles 68
The nagger's quick guide to using a hygrometer 68

WHAT GUIDE WOULD BE COMPLETE WITHOUT RECIPES? 73

BASIC MEAD 75
   Generic Mead Recipe 76

MR. CORSELLISES ANTWERP MEATH 79

MELOMELS 83
Perry-ish Mead 84

MY LORD HOLLIS HYDROMEL 86

All American Mead 88

Huckleberry Mead 90

Vodka mead 92

I Slipped and Fell On My Mead 94

Oak Leaf Meads, stuff like that. 95

SHORT MEAD 96
TO MAKE HONEY DRINK 96

Orange Ginger Mead 98

Ffor to Make Mede. 100

PYMENTS 105
TO MAKE EXCELLENT MEATHE 105

White Pyment 109

Apple Pie Quick Mead 111

METHAGLINS 113
T'ej—Honey Wine 113

METHELIN, OR HONEY WINE. 117

Good mead 119

Roses for My Love 122

Rosemary Ginger Mead 125

Trojniak 128

SACK MEADS 131
STRONG MEAD 131

BOUCHETS 134
  Spicy Bouchet.. 135
  Four Year Bouchet.. 137

THE MAKING OF TISWIN 140
  Oh, the Beer Has Gone Flat? Make Mead!..................... 142

A VERBOSE BIBLIOGRAPHY AND RESOURCE LIST 143

THE PROMISED LIST OF OTHER MEAD TYPES 149

OPENING NOTE

Greetings, one and all. This is the Tim's wife and fellow collaborator in this alcoholic adventure. For the duration of this book, you may call me The Nagger.

When my husband and I first got married, he asked me to redo his mead book entitled *The Knight of Cups* and illustrate it. He had done it to earn his knighthood for a medieval re-enactment game[2], and it was sitting on Lulu.com being completely ignored. (It also had never sold a single copy but seems to have been plagiarized at least twice.)

In those days I had the time, so I said yes. Then I stopped having the time. When I was finally able to look at it, I found out that it was actually no more than a research paper.

---

[2] As much as Tim loves the Society for Creative Anachronism, that's not the one.

This would never do, at least for me. If you say you've written a book, I'm expecting a book. I probably was also the worst person in the world to ask for help in this project, because I have...hold your breath ...a college degree. And it just happens to have something to do with history. And if there's one thing I associate mead with, it's history.

So I found myself giving my husband's paper a complete overhaul. My husband, when he realized the enormity of the work in front of him, became predictably reluctant to do anything. That's how I ended up writing most of this book.

This book is now a completely changed manual: We organized the information, checked spelling, researched, and other important documentation necessities. I transformed into every writer's worst nightmare. I became...*an editor* on top of a co-collaborator.

Ha. Tim thinks he had it difficult. If only he *knew*. Editors, REAL editors, are meaner. MUCH meaner. And they're responsible for paying you, which means you want to make them happy, and they have contracts over you such as you've never seen.[3]

My husband and I scoured what we could find of Medieval, Renaissance and early American documents and collected somewhere along a hundred or more recipes for different types of mead. We almost included them all, but then we realized about 78% of them were from the very same book. That was a bit top-heavy and felt too much like plagiarism, so we instead chose the best recipes from the litter—which necessarily cut the book count down by a ginormous amount. (The books are listed in the bibliography if you wish to find it to get the rest of the recipes.)

And then I sat down and expanded our two paragraph long section on the history and traditions of mead-making, wrapped this book up, and called it a day. =^-^= And yes, it has illustrations.

If you're new to making mead, then we hope this book is for you. This is a how-to book, so most of the

---

[3] He thinks I have a contract called marriage? He thinks this voluntary contract known as the Ol' Ball and Chain is constricting? Wait until you have to fight for your character's personal rights to live for months straight while ignoring your own! And money? At least when *I* get his paycheck, I use it to buy food and feed him! HA!

recipes we picked are the easier kind any beginner can burn well. (Hey, I once burned water. If you can burn water, you can burn anything.) If you are already a veteran in the mead making ways of honey, perhaps this book will contain something you don't know yet. We hope so.

At the very least, I hope my footnotes/endnotes will make you laugh. ☺ Happy mead making!

K. J. Joyner[4]

---

[4] You might have seen me in such conventions as Tsubasacon or Cyphercon.

Mead brewing can be a fun and rewarding hobby that brings a taste of the past back to our current lives. It adds ambiance to a feast and is a much sought after drink for not only medieval events but for any of those that enjoy a good drink that ranges from sweet and slightly alcoholic to dry and very alcoholic.

Much of this is based upon data from either my personal experiences or the experiences of others. The sources I used were various files I acquired through the internet and from local brewers. The recipes are either open source from the internet, my own creation, or historical books.

I thank you for your time and patience.

Timothy Belcher

INTRODUCTION

Byrþi betri berrat maþr brautu at,
an sé manvit mikit;
auþi betra þykkir þat í ókunnun staþ,
slíkt es válaþs vera.

Esa svá gott, sem gott kveþa,
öl alda sunum,
þvít fæ'ra veit, es fleira drekkr,
síns til geþs gumi.

Óminnis hegri heitr sás of ölþrum þrumir,
hann stelr geþi guma;
þess fugls fjöþrum ek fjötraþr vask
í garþi Gunnlaþar.

Ölr ek varþ, varþ ofrölvi
at ens fróþa Fjalars;
því's ölþr bazt, at aptr of heimtir
hverr sitt geþ gumi.

(translation)

*A better burden no man can bear
on the way than his mother wit:
and no worse provision can he carry with him
than too deep a draught of ale.*

*Less good than they say for the sons of men
is the drinking oft of ale:
for the more they drink, the less they can think
and keep a watch over their wits.*

*A bird of Unmindfullness flutters over ale-feasts,
wiling away men's wits;
with the feathers of that fowl I was fettered once
in the garths of Gunnlodr below.*

*Drunk was I then, I was over-drunk,
in the fold of wise Fjalar;
But best is an ale feast when a man is able
to call back his wits at once.*

> Words attributed to Odin, chief of the gods, warning against drinking way too much as we fool mortals love to do.[5]

---

[5] But really, who ever listened to a god? Especially one who liked to hang upside down and sacrifice his eyes over something as silly as wisdom? On the other hand, the female Viking piratess Alfhild—while a goddess of the sea still yet a mortal—kept her ship stocked

THE OBLIGATORY HISTORY AND TRADITION OF MEAD CHAPTER

Woodcut circa 1692-1694

with nothing but mead to drink and an all female crew. So when you virile young males picture those sweaty, fit Vikingesses pulling at those ropes while in that hot, summer sun you can bless mead. That's right. Mead is responsible for everything sexy, my friends. Drink up.

Honey is a divine substance—fruit of the...insects! It's a heavenly color—gold—and tastes just as holy. (That is, if you like honey.) It is the only food that will not spoil, nor will it mold[6]. Honey has medicinal properties and is antibacterial. And where do we get honey from? We get it from stealing from bees. Never again let it be said that drinking isn't a gateway drug to stealing.

Mead is a fermented beverage brewed from honey that has been enjoyed since before the dawn of recorded time. (Nagger's note: Some scholars trace mead's archaeological trail as far back as 7000 BC and it appears to be a worldwide phenomenon. Not only did the European and African cultures have mead, but the Mayans did as well—although that particular recipe we couldn't include into this book due to the hallucinogenic qualities it claims to possess.)

Bees were initially kept in hives made of coiled wicker. (This was a long time ago before the invention

---

[6] This is because honey is mostly comprised of sugar and perhaps a little water. If stored properly, honey stays good for years. If not stored properly one of two things can happen. It turns into crystallized chunks of sugar, or it gets eaten.

of cell phones and motorcars.) To remove the honey, the bees had to be killed and the hive torn apart.[7] As time and skills have progressed, beekeepers have since learned how not to kill the hive and manage to, in fact, cultivate bee colonies for generations. But that was then and this is now.

In those early days when colonies were killed and combs were, well, combed there were several different grades of honey extracted from the hive in various ways. The first of the honey (and the best) would be allowed to seep out. The second in quality would be squeezed out of the wax gently. The third best would come from crushing the comb and the wax.

The final and least desirable honey came from gently boiling all that remained to make honey water, which was then strained off. This was the honey water blend used to make mead for the common man.

From a historical standpoint, we may be very lucky to still know how to make mead the old-fashioned way. Wine, another alcoholic beverage that's just

---

[7] It was the end of the world, and they knew it.

about as old as mead, was the domain of the rich in those early days because of how hard it was to a hold of some good grapes. (California was yet to be invented.) Mead became, as a result, the drink of the common man. Honey wasn't that hard to get, and making mead isn't that difficult. (Which is why we were able to write this book. I hope you didn't take us for geniuses.)

So common man had it made. He made it, drank it, and then made some more. It was a beautiful cycle.

Okay, I have to level with you. This actually wasn't as good for mead as it sounds. Trends aren't set by your common bloke, not even today. I'm sure you wish they were, but even torn jeans only got popular because folks with money noticed the poor kids were looking more cool than usual.

Yes, trends are set by those who set the example. Those that set the example are usually those with the money. Wine, because of its scarcity, was expensive. If given a choice between a bottle of mead and a bottle of wine, your average nose-in-the-air man of the hour was going to choose his wine. This was how the nobleman bragged about his wealth: by showing off how much better his groceries were than yours.[8] The more wine was chosen as a rich man's drink, the less mead made the cut. It's sad. But true.

Common man kept mead going as a local drink of choice, but there would still be more factors rising against mead's survival. There was a point in time when mead drinking really suffered a popular blow, and people reached for other beverages.

One theory why is that the reformation movement with the New Church of England got involved—not in the way you might expect. Yes, we all know about today's prohibition laws and the prudes who prefer to live our lives for us by restricting what we can eat and drink. Even though the Church has been involved with the great prude movements throughout history, it didn't have anything against mead at all. There were no edicts issued banning commoners from drinking this holy golden beverage.

---

[8] Much like today's socialite would drive a humvee, own a yacht, or be caught in a South American hotel with twelve hookers and a smoking pistol.

Instead, candle makers who depended on honey combing to get wax for their candle making ran into a bit of a production slump: their candles weren't as much in demand by the church as they used to be. With less honey combing going on, there was less honey being produced for the slovenly masses. (You'd think it were the other way around, but those old folks seem to have their priorities switched from the rest of us sots.) This meant the cost of mead making rose. Which meant less commoners could afford it. Which meant mead as a drink and tradition took one for the team.

Whether or not this theory is correct, it is also a fact that when Marco Polo—that famous wandering Italian whose memory is kept alive in backyard swimming pools all over America—returned from the Spice Islands he brought a revolutionary new product; sugar cane.

Even today sugar is the dominant sweetener. When you go to make a jug of tea, which do you normally choose to make it taste better: sugar, Splenda, or honey? Well, before sugar you might have said honey but these days you're probably going to reach for that insidious bag of sugar. Honey, being far less in demand now that sugar began its world conquest, fell to the wayside and got more expensive, etc. By now you know the rest of the cycle.

Another thing that went against mead was the growth of civilization itself. Villages grew into town, and those grew into cities. I'm sure you all know what happens when man becomes your typical urban dweller. He stops living off the land and learned to live off the market place.

Picture it. People began to forget how to do things like grow their own vegetables and make their own alcohol. This isn't unlike today, when some people honestly believe meat doesn't comes strictly from the grocery store and have no idea the horrific slaughter farmers commit to get that tasty dead flesh.[9]

If it weren't for the European monasteries that needed the bees as a wax source for candle making, mead making may have died out completely. When

---

[9] On this point, I do not jest.

wax was harvested from the combs, honey was mysteriously still the byproduct. It was the weirdest thing. Who was going to eat and drink all this honey? If no one wanted it, that left the monks: Monks who needed to drink stuff and knew how to cook. Inevitably mead making survived. You may stop to thank God now.

Probably because of its age and origins,

Above: A Norse picture from the 18th century Icelandic manuscript "SÁM 66", which is now in the care of the Árni Magnússon Institute in Iceland. The second eagle is the giant **Suttung**, the first being **Odin**. They are depicted struggling over the tasty Mead of Poetry. This image was found in the Wikimedia Commons website and was picked because the nagger can't read Icelander.

mead has acquired a mystical, magical and healing reputation in our daily lives and mythologies. (It was unavoidable that over time folks would begin to notice that sick people drinking mead got well faster. Or that healthy people drinking mead got drunk. And—they seemed to get healthier.) For example there is the notorious Mead of Poetry[10], a Norse mythological concoction requiring the blood of Ksavir, a wise godly being. Drinking this stuff apparently turned you into a scholar or poet.[11]

Pliny the Elder wrote:

> "Hydromel is recommended, too, as very good for a cough: taken warm, it promotes vomiting. With the addition of oil it counteracts the poison of white lead; of henbane, also, and of the halicacabum, as already stated, if taken in milk, asses' milk in particular. It is used as an injection for diseases of the ears, and in cases of fistula of the generative organs. With crumb of bread it is applied as a poultice to the uterus, as also to tumours suddenly formed, sprains, and all affections which require soothing applications.... After it has been kept a considerable time, it becomes transformed into a wine, which, it is universally agreed, is extremely prejudicial to the stomach, and injurious to the nerves."

---

[10] Old Norse skáldskapar mjaðar

[11] It's only fair to note being drunk often makes people wisely create what they feel are the most important works of all time, usually about the meaning of life in a few verses. Because most are about getting drunk, high or laid one can only conclude the meaning of life is, "You're boned."

Mead has often been sung about—which is probably the greatest tribute mankind can give to anything. You want to know you're awesome? A little mead and a song will prove it to you for the rest of your life. We sing about our lovers, we sing about God (or gods), and we've apparently been singing about mead for almost as long. The first discovered 'recording' is a hymn describing mead from the *Rigveda*, which is a sacred volume from the Vedic and Hindi faiths.[12] Even the famous bard Taliesin wrote a song about it; 'Kanu y med' or 'Song of Mead' around AD 550. All mead needs is for the music to hit the American pop charts and it will simply go virile. Again.

The oldest recorded mead recipe (that we could find) was written by a Roman named Columella around 60 BCE. It was found in a series of books the author wrote titled *De ReRustica*, which were advice to another Roman named Publius Silvinus. I have in-

---

[12] Actually the Rigveda mentions mead more than once, using it as a reference to describe the richness of a holy being's footsteps or being used as a special gift. And I have by no means read the entire thing. I did a quick word search on the document, found the words, was interested, and then real life took me away from my new shiny toy.

cluded it here instead of in the recipe section because this recipe uses wild yeast to ferment the beverage—a process that will more likely kill you than get you drunk (especially in America).

That being said here is the recipe for posterity sake, not for actual use:

> Take rainwater kept for several years, and mix a sextarius of this water with a pound of honey. For a weaker mead, mix a sextarius of water with nine ounces of honey. The whole is exposed to the sun for 40 days, and then left on a shelf near the fire. If you have no rain water, then boil spring water.

When it comes to tradition, some of our modern ones are thanks to mead. The term 'honeymoon' is said to be intertwined with a European custom of drinking honey-based mead for a month (moon) after the wedding. This was to insure that the first child of the union was a male. A firstborn male child was considered lucky.[13] (Oddly enough science has backed

---

[13] Nice romantic story, isn't it? Other interesting versions claimed it comes from the Viking word "hjunottsmanathr", which means "in hiding" and doesn't mention honey at all. The most amusing we found stated it was an ancient Babylonian word that stemmed from

this idea. A high honey diet apparently alters the Ph balance in a woman enough to favor a male child.)[14]

There's also the great tradition of going out drinking with our friends. Where do we go for that? Normally we go to bars (or pubs, depending on where on the planet you are.) We also feast during this drinking foray, if we're smart and like to avoid the ill effects of careless drinking. Enter then, the mead hall.

According to the much disputed Wikipedia, a mead hall is an ancient Scandinavian and Germanic European feasting hall. It was a large building with a single room. The nagger believes this to be true because

---

the holy tradition of the new husband staying properly drunk. To keep things strictly scientific, this verbose footnote is to tell you that the word first officially appears sometime around 1552. Richard Huloet's *Abecedarium Anglico Latinum* gives it the following definition (in modernized spelling): "Honeymoon, a term proverbially applied to such as be new married, which will not fall out at the first, but the one loveth the other at the beginning exceedingly, the likelihood of their exceeding love appearing to assuage, the which time the vulgar people call the honey moon". In other words, it simply refers to one pathetic little month in your marriage when your love is as sweet as honey and ebbs about as fast as doeth the sweetness. Such is etymology. And cynicism. Thank you. I'm here all week.

[14] My husband is a horrible reference keeper, so I hunted a very long time to find any scientific evidence he mentions. The best I can find for this part is an article referencing a study conducted by Exeter University: http://www.ehow.com/way_5451961_diet-conceive-boy.html

there is archaeological evidence as well as Norse accounts and similar writings. Wikipedia for the win.

So interestingly, mead's written history marks it as a golden virtue of the gods—the stuff of poetry and song. When it almost died out, it was saved through the acts of godly servants. And today its reputation remains firm. Pagans place it as a center piece on their altars, Christian men serve it at Christenings, and hearth healers give a cup to cure what ails you.

We the mead makers give bottles away to friends, carry bottles with us to revels to share, and honor that special place the mead hall. It remains the drink of the common man. And somewhere out there, a Norse god is probably chuckling to himself in amusement that his complicated plans to preserve his favorite soft drink have worked ever so well.

All in all, mead itself hasn't changed over the past hundreds of years. And apparently neither have the circumstances around it. So drink up: ambrosia never tasted so sweet.

The Page of Cups

KANU Y MED (SONG OF MEAD)

From the Book of Taliesien XIX

*I WILL adore the Ruler, chief of every place,
Him, that supports the heaven: Lord of everything.
Him, that made the water for every one good,
Him, that made every gift, and prospers it.
May Maelgwn of Mona be affected with mead, and affect us,
From the foaming mead-horns, with the choicest pure liquor,
Which the bees collect, and do not enjoy.
Mead distilled sparkling, its praise is everywhere.
The multitude of creatures which the earth nourishes,
God made for man to enrich him.
Some fierce, some mute, he enjoys them.
Some wild, some tame, the Lord makes them.
Their coverings become clothing.
For food, for drink, till doom they will continue.
I will implore the Ruler, sovereign of the country of peace,
To liberate Elphin from banishment.
The man who gave me wine and ale and mead.
And the great princely steeds, beautiful their appearance,
May he yet give me bounty to the end.
By the will of God, he will give in honour,
Five five-hundred festivals in the way of peace.
Elphinian knight of mead, late be thy time of rest.*

NORSE RIDDLE

I am man's treasure, taken from the woods,
Cliff-sides, hill-slopes, valleys, downs;
By day wings bear me in the buzzing air,
Slip me under a sheltering roof-sweet craft.
Soon a man bears me to a tub. Bathed,
I am binder and scourge of men, bring down
The young, ravage the old, sap strength.
Soon he discovers who wrestles with me
My fierce body-rush—I roll fools
Flush on the ground. Robbed of strength,
Reckless of speech, a man knows no power
Over hands, feet, mind. Who am I who bind
Men on middle-earth, blinding with rage?
Fools know my dark power by daylight.[15]

---

[15] Need a hint? This book has something to do with it. C'mon. Give it some thought...

THE TYPES OF MEAD

Mead. Like a teenager on the internet, it goes by many names. Mostly this is because not everybody speaks English. The word, mead, comes from the Old English word meodu. It's also called honey beer or honey wine.

Being as it's made of honey.

As is the way with humans and their wild cooking experimentations, various types of mead have been developed over the long centuries. Here is a short and sweet list of definitions.

> **Mead** is classified not by the kind of honey that it is made of, but by what other flavors might have been added to it.
>
> **Basic mead** is made with only honey, water, and yeast, plus maybe a small amount of either natural or artificial acid to balance the sweetness.
>
> **Bochet** is made by burning honey, preferably over an open fire. You shouldn't need

marshmallows for this as people have claimed it smells like burned marshmallows or even caramel during the making.

Great mead — Any mead meant to be aged several years—that whole "No wine served before its time" thing. The designation is meant to distinguish this type of mead from "short mead".

Melomel is mead made by adding fruit or fruit juices, or both. (Unless you use only grapes.) Melomel may also contain spices.

Cyser is an apple melomel. You may know it as a cider.

Metheglin is made by adding herbs or spices, like cloves or cinnamon.

Pyment is a melomel made with grapes or grape juice.

Sack is a name (or an adjective) for stronger mead. Depending on the initial amount of honey, and how effective at fermenting the yeast is, the final mead may be dry or sweet. Sack mead is usually sweet.

Short Mead (or "quick mead") is mead that is brewed quicker than traditional mead and generally is finished anywhere from 3 days to a month.

Traditional mead would be any mead (be it a melomel, a ceyser, a bochet, etc.) that is made using only traditional ingredients; nothing modern such as chemical additives and such. Some people go somewhat further and say traditional meads must be made only with historical methods (allowing wild yeast to ferment the brew, using double layers of cloth to keep impurities out, and such).[16]

---

[16] There are some types of mead not listed up there so I'm listing them in the back of the book because they felt left out and lonely. They all protested very loudly and made me feel feelings, so something had to be done. A lot of them could possibly fall under the top listed types I already listed in the list earlier in these pages.

What Kinds of Honey?

> *Nagger's note:* One bit of advice many people thoughtfully offered when they learned this book was being edited for re-release was what type of honey to use. This is what my husband has to say, based on the original text from his book.

There are many kinds of honey, based on which flowers the bees collected the nectar from. (Bees will travel for miles looking for just the right nectar. If you're lucky enough that those miles include most of the same type of blossom, you can get some really good tastes in honey. Among the two most popular are palmetto honey—which I've seen people pay plenty for—and orange blossom honey, which kind of tastes like oranges.) Any characterization of honey as being from a particular source can vary from absolutely true to a rough generality, depending on what flowers the bees can find and how interesting they find them.

Honeys range in taste and color from the light to stronger tasting (and darker).[17] The honey you choose to use depends both on which you like the taste of, and what type of mead you are trying to make. Stronger flavors go well in metheglins and heavier or sweet meads, while the milder honeys make a good base for melomels or dry traditional meads.

You can buy honey in bulk from roadside stands or health food stores. Look in the phone book for honey, health food stores, or beekeepers. Be inventive. (Nagger's note: For example, when purchasing a bulk of honey to be used in photographing illustrations for this book, we ended up purchasing our honey from a guy in Miami we found on Ebay. The honey turned out to be orange honey—which I had never had before but instantly adored.) If there is no other source the grocery store (while a last resort) always has honey.

---

[17] They say the darker honey is the healthiest for you. Come to the dark side.

INCREDIBLY NIFTY LIST OF WAYS TO BUY LOTS AND LOTS OF HONEY:

1. Local beekeepers who are willing to make an extra buck. You can find them by looking up your local bee keepers association through the phone book or the internet.

2. Local health food store

3. Friends, family, and countrymen

4. Crazed internet search (keywords: bulk honey)

5. Ebay.com, Craigslist, Bookoo.com and any local bulletin board

6. Grocery store.

7. Raise your own bees.

The honey can be either raw or processed. What's the difference? I'm glad you asked. Raw honey has not been processed to remove the various impurities that come with all natural products. You have the most control over raw honey.

Honey may be processed to make it clearer, remove impurities, and less likely to crystallize.[18] The more processed it is, the milder it will be and the less character it will give your finished product. Processing also removes some of the honey's aroma. Commercial, grocery store honey is the most processed and the last choice for mead making.

(Nagger's note: Here are two jugs of wildflower honey and apple juice intended for a nice batch of Apple Pie mead. If I were making orange mead, I'd choose orange blossom honey because I'm picky that way, but it's not necessary. What kind of honey you pick will only matter as much as you're willing for it to matter. You're the brewer here, and whether the mead turns out tasty depends more on the brewing process than anything.)

---

[18] Crystallization is when honey goes 'bad.' It actually doesn't go bad, but it can turn into a jar-shaped block of sugar. Avoid this by putting your jar in warm water when things start to crystallize—or use it all making mead. I highly recommend the latter suggestion.

EQUIPMENT FOR BREWING.

There are several things that you will need to brew with. At a minimum:

> A large pot to heat your mixture in. The best pots to use are stainless steel or enameled.
>
> A glass or plastic vessel to allow the mixture to ferment in
>
> Some sort of airlock to prevent unwanted bacteria from invading the mixture.[19]
>
> Stirring implements: make sure they're the kind that won't melt
>
> Some sort of screen (like a fine straining mesh) and/or cheesecloth
>
> Tubing
>
> Yeast, preferably wine yeast

---

[19] Sometimes those bacteria can be worse than huns.

All of your equipment should be food grade plastic, metal or glass (do not use wood, it holds flavors and bacteria).

Figure 1: We are a big pot and a plastic vessel with water.

I recommend somewhere between a 2 and a 5 gallon pot (depending on the size of your brewing batches) for the main cooking process.

There are several options for the fermentation vessel. Food grade plastic buckets work, as do glass or plastic water bottles. As long as you can seal it in such a way to keep unwanted things out while at the same time ing fermentation gasses to pass through, it will work.

Figure 2: You may not recognize me but I'm part of an airlock.

Figure 3: Rejoice for I am an entire airlock.

Airlocks come in a couple of types. (See illustrations) The common ones you can buy from a store are either the "s tube" or a 3 piece that has a plastic cover over the tube that sits in water. In a pinch you can use a balloon with a small hole poked in the top of it.

Various items for stirring are required to mix your blend as you heat it.

Some recipes call for skimming off the scum that forms as you heat the mixture. The best way to do that is with a cheesecloth-lined strainer.

Finally, it is not required but a siphon tube or racking cane will make your brewing experience a lot easier.

Figure 4: This may be a little cheesy, but we are cheesecloth and a straining tool. Together.

Siphoning lets you transfer your mixture from pan to fermentation container or from one fermentation container to the next without a large mess. A racking cane (which is a useful tool made of a piece of rigid plastic tube with some flexible tube attached to it) will have a stopper on the bottom to keep it from sucking most of the gunk that is settled on the bottom of the container into the new container.

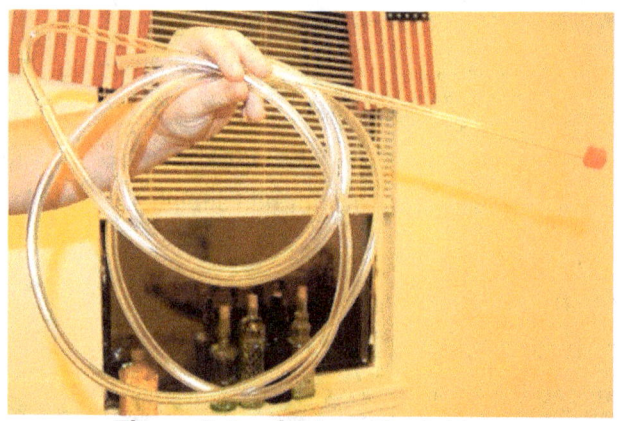

Figure 5: Lo, for I am the tubing.

(Nagger's note: Don't forget the yeast! It's the yeast that makes the mead!! I could tell you how, but you might find it a little gross. Just know ants and their aphids ain't got nothing on you. Okay. I'll tell you later.)

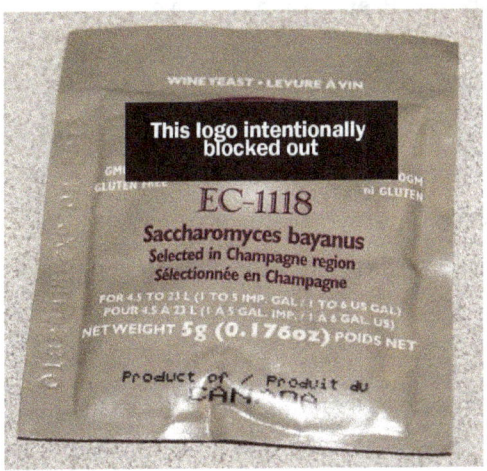

PREPARING THE SACRED NECTAR OF THE GODS

Step One: Preparation for the brewing session.

There are several things that must be done to prepare to brew. They can be simple, they can be difficult, and they're necessary. Get over it now if you want to brew. They don't care if you hate them.

Obviously the ingredients you need are going to be based on your recipe and will vary from time to time. Moving along.

Sanitation is paramount in getting a product that is both tasty and will last. (Not to mention it will keep you and your mead from getting sick.) Before each brewing session you should clean and sterilize any area that your tools will touch. Bleach will do but there are

The Page of Cups

a variety of sterilization agents made specifically for brewing that will work faster and easier.

(Nagger's note: Such agents are a mild anti-bacterial detergent, Oxiclean, and Straight-A. You will also need sponges, elbow grease, and finally cleaning the bedroom floor so that your mate is willing to help you clean the brewing area later.)

Once your area is clean and sterile you need to start with each piece of your equipment and sterilize them. You don't want your labor of love to turn into a poisonous disaster.

Step Two: How to Prepare the Must[20]

Before fermenting, the honey-water mix (which is

based on the ingredients called for in your recipe) is called must. To create the must, you simply mix the ingredients in the pot.

For a basic mead

---

[20] Do what you must but do it right.

you're only going to add the honey and water in the right amounts. (Your recipes will know.) For more complex meads you also add spices, fruits, or whatever else that you may wish to add in the sequence called for by the recipe or your own mad desires.

You have to be careful while heating the must. Heating while adding the honey risks caramelizing any that sticks to the bottom of the pot. (Nagger's note: what that means is the stuck honey might become very thick like soft candy and ruin the must.) Don't heat unless you're absolutely supposed to. Some mead recipes recommend only heating the must enough to pasteurize it (or not at all) to prevent driving off some of the delicate honey flavors.

When heating, don't heat too quickly and stir constantly.

During the heating process, scum is usually going to form on the top of the mixture. When you see it, you'll know it. It will resemble ocean foam or other such foamy stuff that floats on the top of liquid.

If you're me you want it to form, because it's gross stuff. Why do you think you call people scum when they're, well, being scum? Because they're scum.

Scum is made up of all the nasty little impurities found in your base ingredients; mostly your honey.[21]

---

[21] In case you weren't aware of it, honey is essentially bee puke.

When scum develops on the top of the must, you can skim it off with a strainer wrapped in cheesecloth. (Unless you would rather leave it in, some people believe that it adds to the flavor.)

See the next illustrations for photographs of scum being taken from its natural habitat.

(You scum!)

(Above: Gently skimming scum off the top of must.)

Step three: Adding Acid

At this point, what you do next is crucial for fermentation: the process by which the yeast put inside the must feasts on your mixture and creates alcohol.

You add acid to make your yeast feel right at home. Yeast loves acidic environments. It would rather hang out on the curb with its acidic friends taunting the lesser yeasts than meditate at a temple or relax in a calm cafe. You're making alcohol here, so don't expect any Zen wisdom from your yeast. It likes things acidic, period.

Other things do not. The minute things get too acidic, they throw up their microscopic hands and cry, "There goes the neighborhood!" This is a good thing. If your mix is more sweet than acidic, you risk letting all those nasty things that will destroy your blend take root.

Acid is added to the honey water mix to balance the sweetness of the honey and to adjust the ph balance to make the yeast happy. Happy yeast means better fermentation. The added acid will also protect the must until the alcohol level can create a hostile environment for the other microorganisms. You want other microorganisms to go away. Your yeasts are snobs. Cater to that.

Acid can be added in many ways. (Nagger again: I should point out we are NOT talking about lab acid. This is not the stuff that would melt your floor.) Winemaking suppliers sell acid blends, powder or liquid. Acid is measured in 'as tartaric,' or how acidic the blend is in relation to pure tartaric acid.. Acid blends are a combination of tartaric, citric, and malic acids. The natural acid in fruits and berries will also acidify the must. This is why melomel meads often need no additional acid.

If you chose to add brewers acid (instead of acid from a natural source like fruit or some tea) then simply follow the instructions provided on the label.

Step four: Yeasts

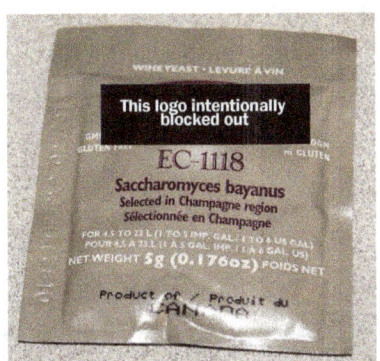

Once again, a picture of the yeast. In case you forgot.

Mead is stronger than a beer, usually more like a wine, with a final alcohol level anywhere between 10 and 18 percent. This is thanks to yeast.

Each yeast imparts its own unique tendencies to the mead. At any rate the type of yeast you choose is entirely up to you. Any yeast (even bread yeast you can get at your local grocer) will work. It's a matter of preference.

Yeast will either come as a liquid or a powder. To add the yeast you have to prepare it and then aerate it into the mixture. If your yeast is a dry or dehydrated yeast (powder) you must rehydrate it.

Generally this involves letting the yeast settle into a quarter cup of warm (not hot) water, with perhaps some sugar to help it get started. If your yeast is already liquid then it is ready to go although it may require some steps to prepare it. Follow the instructions on the package.

It should be noted that some brewers have found using a yeast that is less tolerant to alcohol like Lalvin EC-1118 will produce a sweeter mead.

(The yeast must flow.)

Wine Yeasts

Wine yeasts may start slower but their higher alcohol tolerance will allow them to ferment more completely than ale or lager yeast. Generally they also produce fewer off tastes which will keep your mead on a shelf aging long after it is finished. Some of the more popular yeasts are:

Champagne Tokay

Epernay

Sherry

Steinberg

Flor

Prise De Mousse.

Champagne finishes very dry and has a high alcohol content. Flor Sherry has a flavor that goes well with sack meads, as well as a higher alcohol content. Epernay lends itself to the more fruity meads. Prise de Mousse is particularly neutral and fast.

Bread Yeasts

Bread yeast is the only one that will not have concise instructions because it is not intended for brewing (works just fine, just not what it is intended for). If you choose to use bread yeast then do the following:

Float the yeast in a quarter cup of warm water for 15 min.

Stir vigorously until mixed.

Adding the Yeast:

Before adding your yeast, you first want to transfer your must to whatever vessel you will be allowing the mixture to ferment in. (Nagger's note: You can do this in a lot of creative ways, but we have found that siphoning is the quickest, easiest, and helps filter out some of the impurities.)

Make sure it is about room temperature before you add the yeast—if your must is too hot it can kill your yeast.

To siphon, off insert a tube (such as a racking cane) into the liquid (keeping it above the level of your fermentation vessel) and suck on the other end as you would a straw. Do this until the liquid starts to flow. (Nagger's note: be quick or you may end up with a mouth full of gas—I mean, unfermented mead.)

Siphoning the mead.

Stick the hose into the fermentation vessel and allow the suction of the moving fluid to pull the rest of the mixture through the hose. Either swallow the liquid that is in your mouth or spit it into the sink, not back into your mixture.

Once it is all in there and at the right temperature just pour your yeast gently into the mixture, shake it up to make sure things are mixed well, and cap with the airlock of your choice.

Step Five: Fermentation

Fermentation is the process of yeast giving off waste. Hey, we all give off waste. Some of us do it more than others. Why should yeast be the exception?

Yeast is a microorganism that must eat, and it loves sugar like what you find in honey. As it eats, it produces alcohol and carbon dioxide. Obviously we drink the alcohol. The carbon dioxide bubbles into the air to escape, which is why you need an airlock.

There's a formula to this process. If the yeast were fermenting glucose (sugar) it would look something like $C_6H_{12}O_6 \rightarrow 2\ C_2H_5OH + 2\ CO_2$.

However, this book isn't written for chemists so try not to panic at those chemical compounds. You only need to understand that yeast eats, yeast gives off waste, and without an airlock your fermentation container would probably explode. Yeast doesn't care to stop putting out waste just because you forgot to give its gas a place to go.

Mead fits no set category when it comes to fermentation and time. Mead likes to ferment at warm temperatures, roughly 70 to 80 degrees. If it gets too cold, the yeast can go dormant which means fermentation crawls to a halt. On the other hand it should be stored in a cool place after bottling.

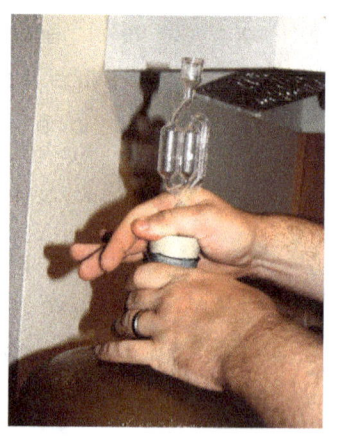

Capping the fermentation vessel with airlock.

Sometimes at this stage in mead making you can

accidentally kill your yeast, especially if you make a mistake in storage temperature. Don't worry. You can add more yeast if it's dead.

If you think your yeast is dead because you put your fermentation vessel in an area that was too cold, don't panic until you know for sure. Simply move the vessel to some place warmer and wait 24 hours. If you have a balloon with a hole in it over the airlock, you'll be able to tell if your yeast has went active again. The balloon will once again fill with carbon dioxide.

> (Nagger's note: To keep the peace, when you have your mead bottled and the airlock secured in place, stash your smelly jugs of brew some place that's neither too cold nor too hot. Did I mention you should put it out of the way?)

Racking the mead

Racking is simply transferring the mixture (as you did to put it into the fermentation vessel) from one container into another (cleaned and prepped) container. (Nagger's note: This means you get the joy of siphoning the mixture again and again and again.)

You may have to rack mead several times while fermenting to leave behind the sediment and ensure clarity. For nontraditional mead it is recommended to rack about a week into fermentation to remove the bits of fruit and spices that tend to settle out. During your fermentation (especially the longer ones) rack periodically (every 3-4 weeks) to improve clarity and flavor by removing the dead yeast and other detritus that has sunk to the bottom.

Don't be surprised if it takes a day or two (or longer) to see activity in your fermentation process. You can see this activity (once the fermentation process has really gotten started) by watching the bubbles in your airlock (or if you're using a balloon, it should be somewhat taut and leaking c02 out of the pinhole you poked in it.) If you do not see any activity after a week you could have a bad batch of yeast. You can try to add another package of yeast or give it more time.[22].

---

[22] One wonders at this point what would happen if you added a package of wine yeast and then a package of bread yeast: would there be a little race war happening in your fermentation vessel?

Step Six: Stopping fermentation (the horror)

Should you want to stop the fermentation process early there are a few ways you can do it.

Freezing the mead will kill 95-99 percent of the yeast. But if all you do is freeze it you run the risk of it restarting once it warms back into fermenting temperatures. (Nagger's note: In laymen's terms, not all of the yeast freezes to death and will revive when things go back to being comfortable for them.)

Pasteurization will kill the yeast but be careful not to evaporate off the alcohol or distill your mead into something considerably stouter. To pasteurize your mead seal the bottle and bathe it in hot water (150-175 degree's) until the temperature of your mead is at least 150 degrees for an hour or more

Potassium sorbate (when used properly) will prevent the yeast from reproducing so it will keep an already stopped fermentation from restarting.

Would the wine yeasts take over the world, forcing the bread yeasts into their gas-producing servitude? Which of the two yeasts would end up on yeast reservations, barely surviving on a scrap of sugar? Would it all fall down like Ancient Rome—or worse yet, explode the jug in one tasty nuclear explosion?

And a final method is to *filter the mixture* through a .5 micron filter which will remove all the yeast from the mixture.

Step Seven: Bottling Your Brew

What you need:

> Empty and very clean (sanitized) bottles
>
> Corks for said bottles
>
> Corking machine or simple elbow-cranked tool
>
> Your racking cane and hose

By far, putting your delicious brew into their little homes has got to be the most rewarding part of the entire process. You're finished, done, and ready to share with friends and family! Well, almost.

First, and this is pretty important: MAKE SURE THE MEAD HAS STOPPED FERMENTING.[23]

Mead can ferment very slowly, so if you are not entirely sure and the process continues after you have

---

[23] Apparently when the author made his first brew, he bottled it only a few hours after setting it aside to ferment. When he tried to serve the mead at couple of weeks later, the bottles exploded in a fury of fizz that left less than an inch of liquid in each bottle.

bottled it, your risks go from minor (turning a still mead into a sparkling one) to major (having a bottle explode in your hand or face)

'Bottle mines' aren't funny. They're unpredictable and dangerous.

As mead finishes fermenting, the cloudiness will start to settle out. Being clear is not enough though. To be completely sure, use a hydrometer or a yeast killer.

So your mead has definitely finished fermenting. You're good to go. Now what? This is the fun part—and the tricky part. You have to figure out how to get your mead from that big fermentation vessel into those tiny bottles without spilling it all over the kitchen floor and inciting the rage of your household nagger.

This is where your racking cane and hose comes in.

If you're clever like the author, you will simply and gently[24] put your (heavy) fermentation vessel up on the counter and your bottles on a slightly lower plane.

---

[24] You should handle the mead very gently at all times by this point.

Then you siphon the juice from the large vessel into each bottle and—this is the most important part—clean up the mess before the Nagger comes home from shopping.

Other people will rack their mead into an open bucket, gently place it on a higher level surface, and then rack the mead into the intended bottles. And somewhere out there is a guy with no racking cane and hose who simply pours his mead into his bathtub and dips his bottles in to fill them the old-fashioned way. I don't recommend you try that last method: your mead needs to be treated carefully and lovingly for starters. You don't want impurities and filth in your mead for seconds. You stand to lose mead in the wash for thirds.

Your racking cane is your line, so to speak. Use it and you're avoiding all three of those problems as best as possible. Just remember what you learned or already knew about siphoning and you're good to go.

Don't fill the bottles to the very brim with your mead. Leave some room for a cork. Only fill until the mead is a little less than halfway up the neck of the bottle. If you're in doubt about how much mead should be in a single bottle, go to the store and examine the wine bottles there. That's the gap you're aiming to achieve.

Now it's time to put a cork in that...well it's not a bung-hole. Bung-holes, despite what certain popular cartoon shows may suggest, are primarily for barrels. And it's time to put a cork in it.

We use a manual corking machine for our bottles. It's not hard providing you have the right corks for the job. Chamfered #9 corks are one of the recommended kinds.

To cork, insert the cork into the corking machine, place it on top of the bottle and use the handles to lower the plunger forcing the cork into the neck of the bottle.

Except for one last important part: labeling your mead.

You don't have to, but if you experiment with seasons, honeys, and flavors the way we do then you're going to want to have something on that bottle telling you what that strange radioactive concoction you have in the closet is.

How you label them is up to you. I highly recommend you do this, though. Imagine if you accidentally gave your friend raspberry mead instead of the apple vanilla, and your friend was deathly allergic to raspries!

How you label your bottles is up to you, but you definitely want to consider using waterproof label paper you can purchase from the internet. Otherwise, transporting your mead can get slightly tricky if you want to pack the bottles in ice to keep them cool. The condensation can really tear up your pretty labels.

This pretty label was destroyed by condensation! Don't let this happen to you.

Final thoughts on the matter:

Make sure the strength of the bottle matches the

pressure the mead can produce. Sparkling mead will require a sturdy bottle. Beer bottles should be crown capped. American sparkling wine bottles can be crown-capped much like beer bottles.

Still meads may be bottled in regular wine bottles with standard corks, or in crown-capped bottles as above. With still meads the pressure is not an issue; almost any bottle with a good seal will do.

Remember when choosing your bottles that appearance is a good portion of the first impression. If you want to share your mead, you want people to eyeball that bottle and go "Oooh, that looks tasty." So pick bottles that show off the mead's golden color or attract the eye in some way.

Store the bottles in a cool dark place, not the trunk of your car. Not the middle of the dining room table. Nor anywhere that will annoy the Nagger.

THE HANDY DANDY LIST

TO ACQUIRING

COPIOUS AMOUNTS OF BOTTLES

1. Purchase them in bulk through the internet

2. Make friends with your local bar and offer to help them dispose of the empty bottles.

3. Constantly scour yard sales and antique stores for bottles

4. Make lots of alcoholic friends

5. Get donations from locals who would like to sample your mead.

THE NAGGER'S QUICK GUIDE

TO USING A HYGROMETER

Hi folks, it's me again: the Nagger. While going through my husband's glorious book I kept running into questions. One such question was, "Hydrometer?" What the hell is a hydrometer?

As my husband was in bed and blissfully unaware of my confusion, I took it upon myself to look it up.

The following is an explanation of what I found.

A hydrometer is, basically, a tool for checking liquid gravity.[25] Usually they're a sealed glass tube with a weight of some kind at the bottom and a scale printed along the glass neck.

By reading your liquid's gravity, it's essentially telling you how much crap is in your water: mud, bee puke, illicit drugs, etc. Place your hydrometer in a glass of plain water and it will read a density of 1.00. Place your hydrometer in a glass of muddy water, and it will read something else.

So obviously hydrometers aren't used specifically for mead and wine making…but you gotta admit that's one handy dandy use for it. But how does using a hydrometer help with the mead making process? You ask. Well you've probably figured out at least half of it by now, but I'll tell you anyway: it's a way for you to monitor the "cooking" process as time goes by.

When you first make your must and things are fresh and new, take a hydrometer reading. It should

---

[25] So the next time your glass of water asks, "Does this cup make me look fat?", you can test it to find out the truth.

be somewhere around 1.06 to 1.12—keep in mind that this number will vary for your must according to what strange ingredients (especially honey) you added in your wild frenzy of thinking outside of the alcoholic box.

While the yeast is doing its job and your mead ferments, you give it a hydrometer reading about once a week. The liquid gravity should be falling at a somewhat steady rate during this time.

The numbers won't necessarily drop by huge increments. For example, if you start with a liquid gravity of 1.12 you won't suddenly see a drop to 1.00 or anything like that. But you should see some sort of a drop; 1.12 to 1.11 for example.

You're watching your liquid gravity to get an idea of when your mead is complete. (I picture the hydrometer like a little timer. Ding! Fries are done.) Some numbers you want to watch for are:

Dry Mead: 0.099 to 1.006
Medium Mead: 1.006 to 1.015
Sweet Mead: 1.012 to 1.020
Dessert Mead: 1.02 +

If your liquid gravity stops dropping before you reach those numbers, chances are that your yeast went dormant and the batch stopped fermenting. You may need to reactivate it.

Now you're asking me, "So how do I use this stinking thing anyway?" It depends on the hydrometer, to be honest. If they come with instructions, I highly recommend you read them. Instructions are NOT always for weenies.

With most you just put it into the mead and look at it. Think of it as a gravity thermometer or one of those water buoys you see that tell you what the water level is and if you should be leery of tidal surges.

"Why do I want to bother with one of those things exactly?" If you're like my husband, you don't want to bother. He doesn't use one unless he wants to be picky. If you're like me and you want to aim for a very specific type of mead (i.e. dessert mead) then having one of those suckers makes life a little easier. And all the little tavern patrons are happy.

"Okay, well, I've got this jug of fermenting mead. I've got my hydrometer. I've also got this stopper and airlock in the way. What do I do now, smart gal?"

One source suggested you use a "wine thief". Sounds pretty good to me. There are plenty of alcoholics out there hoping to steal my wine I'm sure. (Actually, no. A wine thief is a tool to extract some mead through your stopper.)

My husband will actually remove the stopper and airlock to tweak the jug and make sure things are going smoothly—and obviously you have to remove the stopper when you're racking your batch of mead. So you'll have ample opportunity to ask your mead if it's feeling fat lately[26]. Don't you worry.

---

[26] Here's hoping you're actually reading the footnotes.

WHAT GUIDE WOULD BE COMPLETE WITHOUT RECIPES?

We're finally down to the fun part of this book: the recipes! Each of these recipes we chose were the best of our large collection and chosen for tradition, ease, and overall flavor. Some of our own making, and the rest are adapted from Medieval, early American, and other open domain texts.

One of our sources also mentions several recipes that include wormwood (most known for absinthe). These are noted as an interesting piece of our

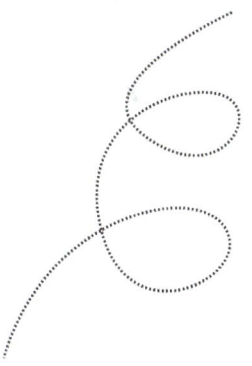

history but not included because we would rather not have someone ingest enough thujone to send them to Valhalla and then have their relatives charge us for the trip.

Each of these recipes may not list all of the steps we talked about in this book. They're only guidelines and not iron shod rules from the gods, so remember what this book has taught you and have fun trying them out!

BASIC MEAD

By definition basic mead is nothing more than honey, water, and something to make it ferment. The ratio of each is a matter of taste. They say true basic mead is fairly rare and hard to find.[27]

The origins of mead can be traced back to the African bush more than 20,000 years ago. Feral bees were well established, elephants roamed the continent and weather patterns were seasonal, as they are today in Africa. Extreme conditions of drought during the dry season, and torrential rains in the rainy season were common. This weather pattern would eventually cause hollows to rot out the crown of the Baobab and Miombo trees, where the elephant had broken branches. During the dry season, the bees would nest

---

[27] Which of course meant that when I asked my husband to make a basic mead for our first brew, he made a melomel.

in these hollows, and during the wet season the hollows would fill with water. Water, honey, osmotolerant yeast, and time and *viola*—a mead is born. Early African bushmen and tribes gathered not only honey, but also mead and as successive waves of people left Africa they possibly took with them some knowledge of mead and mead making.

Generic Mead Recipe

Ingredients:

> 1 gallon honey (which is approximately 11 pounds)
>
> 4 gallons water,
>
> Yeast (it is a matter of personal preference as to whether you use liquid yeast or dehydrated.) I would recommend Champaign or wine yeast, not beer or ale

Instructions:

In a 5 gallon pot add 2 gallons of the water and the honey.

Place on high heat

Stir the honey water until the honey is blended into the water and not stuck to the bottom of the pan.

Boil gently.

As the honey water is boiled a white scum will start to rise to the surface.

Skim the scum off the top until no more is formed.

Remove from heat and allow to cool to a point where it is comfortable for you to handle.

Pour the honey water mix into your fermentation container along with the other 2 gallons of water.

Follow the instructions: on the package for preparing your yeast

Once the yeast is prepared and the honey water is cooled to a point where it is comfortable to handle, add the yeast to the fermentation container and stopper the container with an airlock.

Initially the fermentation will probably be slow. Sugar can be added with the yeast to help kick start the fermentation and will not change the flavor.

In 3 weeks siphon the liquid off the dregs at the bottom into a second fermentation container. At that time taste your brew and if you are happy with it you can either drink it as is or use a yeast killer to kill off the yeast and bottle.

If you are not happy with it stopper it back up with your airlock and let it ferment merrily, checking every 2-4 weeks until you are happy with the taste and alcohol content.

If you like it sweeter use 2 gallons of honey for 5 gallons

MR. CORSELLISES ANTWERP MEATH

This is an old recipe from *The Closet of Sir Kenelm Digby*[28] that's quite popular for a basic mead, or "meath." We quickly figured out it's one of the most popular because the recipe is simple; the mead is true, and well. I'd say it tastes good, but that's also partly due to the brewer.

When it came to this and other old recipes, we hit a slight moral dilemma: do we keep the written language the same in the Old English or do we translate them and make them easier to understand? We finally decided to make them easier to understand because this book is more about learning to make mead and

---

[28] The Closet of the Eminently Learned Sir Kenelme Digbie Kt Opened: Whereby is Discovered Several ways for making of Metheglin, Sider, Cherry-Wine, &c. together with Excellent Directions for Cookery: As also for Preserving, Conserving, Candying, &c. First edition, London, 1669.

Butler, Charles. The Feminine Monarchie, or, A Treatise Concerning Bees and the Due Ordering of Them. Oxford: Joseph Barnes, 1609. May 12, 2012.

Furnivall, Frederick James . Meals and Manners in Olden Time. London : Published for the Early English Text Society by H. Milford, Oxford University Press. 1868

Hartman, George *The Family Physitian*. Pages 492-497: Meads, Metheglin & Hydromel, Wellington, London

following some established recipes than it is reprinting books from the times of yore.

However, we highly recommend you get your own copies of *The Closet of Sir Kenelm Digby* and others—many of which are open domain in places like Project Gutenberg—and enjoy them yourself.

Ingredients:

For every 4 pints of water use two pounds of honey—"To make good Meath, a good white and thick Marsilian or Provence-honey is best. You will need two pounds. Four Holland Pints of water. (the Holland Pint is very little bigger than the English Wine-pint:)"

Instructions:

Stir the honey into the water. "The Honey must be stirred in Water, till it be all melted; If it be stirred about in warm water, it will melt faster."

When all is dissolved, it needs to be strong enough that an egg can float in it with the end up. If it be too sweet or too strong, because there is too much Honey; then you must put more water to it: once again see if the egg floats with the point up.

Don't forget to keep stirring until things are well mixed.

If the egg sinks (which is a token that there is not honey enough) then you must put more Honey to it, and stir about, "till it be all dissolved, and the Eggs swim, as above said."

Now, put your mead over heat such as a stove flame or, if you want to go really traditional, hang it "over the fire".

When you first put the honey over heat, measure how deep the pot or kettle is or measure how much must you have. Boil it until one third of the mixture has boiled away.

When the water begins to seethe (boil), scum will start to form on the top. This must be skimmed off.

When it is thus boiled, it must be poured out into a Cooler, or open vessel, before it be put into your Barrel. (Allow to cool until room temperature.) Something used previously for Sack mead is best. The Bung-hole must be left open, that it may have vent. (Remember your stopper and airlock!)

MELOMELS

Melomels are one of the most numerous types of mead. You can make a melomel from just about any fruit or combination of fruits, so when it comes to this type of mead don't be afraid to let your imagination run wild!

The author has an amusing story about one such melomel his ex-wife decided to make. She combined strawberry, banana and kiwi. He claims the fermentation was so wild, it blew the carboy twice and the mead came out about 70 proof. That was some mead!

Perry-ish Mead

This mead is based on the traditional Roman recipe for perry, which is essentially pear mead.

Ingredients:

5 lbs pears

11 lbs honey (1 gallon)

4 gallons water

1 lb raisins

Yeast

Instructions:

Boil the honey and water until no more scum rises, just as you would for a basic mead.

While allowing the must to cool, cut the pears into slices and put them into your fermentation vessel with the raisins. When your must is about room temperature, put it into the fermentation vessel.

Add yeast as per instructions.

Stopper your vessel with an airlock. Allow the must to ferment until fermentation stops naturally. Once fermentation has finished taste for sweetness.

If it is not sweet enough, boil 1 quart of honey in 1 quart of the wine or water. Add this to the fermentation vessel. Rack every few months and let stand until the taste mellows to the flavor of your choice.

MY LORD HOLLIS HYDROMEL

This is also an old recipe from *The Closet of Sir Kenelm Digby.*

Ingredients:

   4 gallons water

   11 lbs honey (1 gallon)

   1/4th cup sliced ginger, divided into two halves

   1/4th cup rosemary

   1/2 cup sweet-briar leaves[29]

   Yeast

Instructions:

Mix your honey and water together and boil as you would for a basic mead. When no more scum rises to the top and you have skimmed it clean, add one half

---

[29] Sweet briar (Rosa rubiginosa) is originally a European plant, but it has spread across the world. It resembles a rambling rose, but with fewer petals. If you can't find sweet briar, use rose petals as a substitute.

of the ginger. Add the rosemary and the sweet briar leaves. Boil the must for another 15 minutes or so.

Allow the must to cool as you would for basic mead and siphon it into your fermentation vessel.

Add your yeast as per Instructions:

When stoppering with the airlock hang the remaining ginger in a muslin bag from the stopper. Allow to sit for a year before bottling and drinking.

That's right, a full year. There will be no rush drunks on this one!

All American Mead

This particular recipe is an American version preserved in the *Practical Brewer and Tanner* and calls for hops, an ingredient many believe to be strictly the domain of beer. There are those, the author included, who do not believe any mead made with hops is, in fact, mead. And then there are those that feel hops are perfectly acceptable. Indeed, they were including hops in mead as far back as 1555. One such recipe was called "Lithuanian mead" and was used for toasts at weddings. The writer of this book in 1815 apparently also felt that was the way to go.

Ingredients:

    4 gallons of water

    11 lbs honey (1 gallon)

    1 lemon (sliced)

    A handful of powdered ginger[30]

---

[30] Actually the recipe calls for "raced ginger"—not being a French chef, the nagger took it upon herself to figure out what that meant. After a long, boring trial going through dictionaries and websites searches that talked only about racial bigotry and ginger-haired

1 oz hops

Yeast

Instructions:

Mix everything in your pot and boil for 30 minutes. Just with every other mead, skim the scum that rises to the surface of your must. The recipe says for you to do this carefully, so you probably should be a little more careful than usual. Just in case.

Transfer to your fermentation vessel after being allowed to cool

Add yeast, and then stopper your vessel with an airlock

Let sit for 3-4 weeks. (That's it? Not a whole year??)

Bottle after fermentation has stopped.

---

mixed race babies, she finally found one tiny little entry that told her what she needed. Now she's telling you, to stop this racist madness.

Huckleberry Mead

Huckleberries! The nagger's favorite fruit! So rare, so hard to find, so in need of caring people with back yards to propagate the bush back into mainstream culture again!

This recipe calls for a bit more honey than usual—huckleberries can be a bit on the tart side...

Ingredients:

    22 lbs honey (2 gallons)

    3 gallons water

    1 lb huckleberries.

    A handful of vanilla beans. (You can substitute with vanilla extract, but don't use a whole handful. Try a tablespoon or two.)

    Champaign yeast

Instructions:

Boil your must up just as you would for basic mead. Add your huckleberries at end of boil, and let the must stand until it cools.

Pour the mixture into your fermentation vessel and add your vanilla and yeast.

The nagger recommends you let this mixture stand about three months before giving it a try.

Vodka mead

This mead is the result of a conversation between the nagger and her father, who also used to make a lot of mead in his youth.

Ingredients:

- 6 potatoes cut into squares
- 22 lbs honey (2 gallons)
- 3 gallons water
- Yeast

Instructions:

Boil the honey and 2 gallons of water together until no more scum rises. (Basically make your basic mead.)

Boil the potatoes in the final gallon of water until they're soft, then mash potatoes in the water (do not drain).

When all is cool, add them together into the fermentation vessel.

Add your yeast and put on the stopper just like you would basic mead.

Allow to ferment until complete.

Rack every 3 months and allow the mixture to age for about a year.

I Slipped and Fell On My Mead

This basic melomel recipe is the Nagger's father's personal recipe and a favorite. His remark was simply, "Oh, what a flavor."

Ingredients:

22 lbs honey (2 gallons)

5 banana peels

3 gallons water

Yeast

Instructions:

Make your mead just as you would for your basic mead. When the must is cooled and in the fermentation vessel, add your banana peels. Stop with an airlock and allow to ferment for 3 to 6 months.

At 3 months, transfer to a secondary fermentation vessel and strain out the banana peels.

Allow to sit for 6 months before you bottle.

Oak Leaf Meads, stuff like that.

As a final note for melomels, they're not all made from just fruit as you have seen. There are claims that a traditional welsh recipe—which is copyrighted so the Nagger has her doubts on just how old the tradition may be—uses oak leaves as a bittering agent. Another recipe calls for beat roots.

Don't be afraid to try new combinations. Hopefully you're not just getting into mead making to drink. (You could just buy stuff cheaply from the store to do that.) Mead making is an art which produces masterpieces you can only enjoy once. So be artistic!

SHORT MEAD

TO MAKE HONEY DRINK

Another old recipe from *The Closet of Sir Kenelm Digby!*

By now the nagger begins to notice how many modern day recipes call for twice as much honey as Sir Digby and his recipe collaborators felt necessary. In this society where we put sugar in just about everything, it comes as no surprise...but perhaps there's a lesson to be learned from the notion!

Ingredients:

    1/2 gallon water

    1 lb honey

    4-5 cloves per bottle

4-5 thin slices of ginger per bottle

Yeast

Instructions:

Boil the honey and the water together for 45 minutes. As the scum rises skim it off gently. After boiling allow to cool until room temperature and transfer to your fermentation vessel.

Add your yeast and stopper with an airlock.

After 2 weeks stop the fermentation. You can let the fermentation to continue if you wish for your mead to be dryer. Bottle in wine bottles.

In each bottle place 5 cloves and 5 thin slices of ginger.

Seal your bottles and allow them to age.

Drink after a month or two but the longer it waits the better.

Orange Ginger Mead

Some people feel that orange ginger mead is an excellent substitute for champagne. This old recipe, also from Digby, is excellent to serve at that medieval wedding.

Ingredients:

1/2 gallon water

3 lbs honey (1 quart)

1 tablespoons ginger

1/2 tablespoon orange zest. (That would be the peel, grated)

Yeast

Instructions:

Mix the honey and the water. Boil until the mix is reduced by 1/3rd.

While boiling remove the scum that rises to the surface.

After approximately 30 minutes add the ginger and

orange zest. Then remove from the fire. Allow to cool to room temperature.

Once cooled transfer to your fermentation vessel and add your yeast.

This will be ready to drink in 2 to three days but better after a month or two.

If you do not stop your fermentation before bottling remember to use a bottle that can withstand the pressure of carbonation and do not let go longer than a month.

Ffor to Make Mede.

This is taken from *Tractatus de Magnetate et Operationibus Eius*, a 14th century European document, and is one of the oldest known surviving English mead recipes. It's also one of the most popular and can be found all over the internet! Since by now you should know how to make mead, we have left the original Anglo-Saxon for your delight (or not) and put a Nagger's Modern English translation after.

Although it seemed everyone was more than eager to translate the first part on the actual process of making mead, no one wanted to bother with figuring out just what herbs the guy was talking about. This wasn't that hard to do, and it was done, yay verily.[31]

---

[31] For the Nagger's family comes from the deep hills of Kentucky and she grew up reading REALLY OLD books! And her linguistics professor once gave her many red marks on a paper for using 'Old English' phrases because, apparently, that's a completely dead language. The fact that the Nagger grew up speaking that way could not have happened in a million years, she supposes. Except she did.

Tak .1. galoun of fyne hony and to þat .4. galouns of water and hete þat water til it be as lengh þanne dissolue þe hony in þe water. thanne set hem ouer þe fier & let hem boyle and ever scomme it as longe as any filthe rysith þer on. and þanne tak it doun of þe fier and let it kole in oþer vesselle til it be as kold as melk whan it komith from þe koow. than tak drestis of þe fynest ale or elles berme and kast in to þe water & þe hony. and stere al wel to gedre but ferst loke er þu put þy berme in. that þe water with þe hony be put in a fayr stonde & þanne put in þy berme or elles þi drestis for þat is best & stere wel to gedre/ and ley straw or elles clothis a bowte þe vessel & a boue gif þe wedir be kolde and so let it stande .3. dayes & .3. nygthis gif þe wedir be kold And gif it be hoot wedir .1. day and .1. nyght is a nogh at þe fulle But ever after .1. hour or .2. at þe moste a say þer of and gif þu wilt have it swete tak it þe sonere from þe drestis & gif þu wilt have it scharpe let it stand þe lenger þer with. Thanne draw it from þe drestis as cler as þu may in to an oþer vessel clene & let it stonde .1. nyght or .2. & þanne draw it in to an oþer clene vessel & serve it forth

And gif þu wilt make mede eglyn. tak sauge .ysope. rosmaryne. Egre- moyne./ saxefrage. be- tayne./ centorye. lunarie/ hert- is tonge./ Tyme./ marubium album. herbe jon./ of eche of an handful gif þu make .12. galouns and gif þu mak lesse tak þe less of herbis. and to .4. galouns of þi mater .i. galoun of drestis.

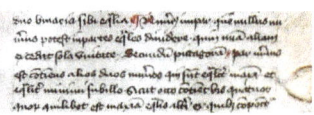

Take 1 gallon of fine honey and to that 4 gallons of water, and heat that water 'til it be as length (possibly boiling) then dissolve the honey in the water.

Then set them over the fire and let them boil and ever skim it as long as any filth rises thereon. And then take it down off the fire and let it cool in other vessel til it be as cold as milk when it comes from the cow.

Then take the dregs (the lees) from the finest ale[32]

---

[32] He's possibly saying to skim the scum from the top, the scum being a type of refuse that drestis would refer to. To take the dregs from the finest ale would be to rack the ale and thus take the finest ale from the dregs. Because you would still be cooking at this point,

or else yeast and cast it into the water and the honey. And stir all well together, but first look before you put thy[33] yeast in that the water with the honey be put in a fair stand and then put in thy yeast or else the dregs for that is best and stir well together. And lay straw or else cloths about the vessel and above if the weather is cold and so let it stand 3 days and 3 nights if the weather is cold. And if it be hot weather, 1 day and 1 night is enough at the full. But ever after 1 hour or 2 at the most assay (sample) thereof and if you will have it sweet take it the sooner from the lees and if you will have it sharp let it stand the longer therewith. Then draw it from the lees as clear as you may into another vessel clean and let it stand 1 night or 2 and then

---

the logical meaning seems more likely. Of course, this can be very debatable on what the author truly wanted you to do. Men aren't any more logical than women are, and we're talking about a recipe from a guy who didn't speak Modern English and may very well have been talking about some other process no one remembers to this day—although a quick trip studying how wine is made suggests the winemakers know. The Nagger doesn't know! Educated guesses are fine, but debates aren't going to bring the man back to life to explain his recipe to us any time soon. Moving along.

[33] Thanks to churches all across the globe, the word 'thy' isn't dead yet. Which means the Nagger chose to use it in this redaction. She hates to see a good thing die. And Old English is a dead language.

draw it into another clean vessel and serve it forth.

And if you would make mead again, take sage, hyssop, rosemary, agrimony, sassafrass, Bethany, centaury, moonwort, hart's tongue, thyme, white horehound, Saint John's Wort. Of each of a handful this you make 12 gallons and if you make less take the less of the herbs and to 4 gallons of the water 1 gallon of dregs.

PYMENTS

TO MAKE EXCELLENT MEATHE

Another old recipe from *The Closet of Sir Kenelm Digby.* Do you get the feeling he's everywhere? More to the point, his book is probably the fattest mead recipe book of all time—or it would be if it were formatted properly. If it weren't for his tireless work collecting recipes they probably would have died with their makers, so we owe Sir Digby hearty thanks.

This recipe also has been translated.

Ingredients:

1 gallon water
3 lbs honey (1 quart)
1 pound raisins
Yeast

Instructions:

Place water in a large pot, then measure with a ruler how high the water is in the pot. Mark your measurement either on the ruler or write it down.

Place on heat. Once water is warm add honey. Let cook.

Skim off the scum as it rises until it stops rising. Now add the raisins.

Once the raisins are thoroughly swollen and soft, remove them and squeeze out all the liquid into a bowl or similar container. Return the liquid to your mixture.

Boil your mixture until the liquid is once again at the level it was when you first measured it.

Transfer your mixture by straining it through a cheesecloth as you put it into a cooling vessel.

Once the mixture is cool, transfer it to your fermentation vessel and add your yeast. Stopper with an airlock and let ferment for 6 weeks.

At 6 weeks test for taste and alcohol content. If you're satisfied, make sure the fermentation is complete and bottle. Hide it for at least 9 months and allow it to age. Don't forget where you've hidden it.

"To every quart of Honey, take four quarts of water. Put your water in a clean Kettle over the fire, and with a stick take the just measure, how high the water cometh, making a notch, where the superficies toucheth the stick. As soon as the water is warm, put in your Honey, and let it boil, skiming it always, till it be very clean; Then put to every Gallon of water, one pound of the best Blew-raisins of the Sun, first clean picked from the stalks, and clean washed. Let them remain in the boiling Liquor, till they be throughly swollen and soft; Then take them out, and put them into a Hair-bag, and strain all the juice and pulp and substance from them in an Apothecaries Press; which put back into your liquor, and let it boil, till it be consumed just to the notch you took at first, for the measure of your water alone. Then let your Liquor run through a Hair-strainer into an empty Woodden-fat, which must stand endwise, with the head of the upper-end out; and there let it remain till the next day, that the liquor be quite cold. Then Tun it up into a good Barrel, not filled quite full, but within three or four fingers breadth; (where Sack hath been, is the best) and let the bung remain open for six weeks with a double bolter-cloth lying upon it, to keep out any foulness from falling in. Then stop it up close, and bdrink not of it till after nine months.

This Meathe is singularly good for a Consumption, Stone, Gravel, Weak-sight, and many more things. A Chief Burgomaster of Antwerpe, used for many years to drink no other drink but this; at Meals and all times, even for pledging of healths. And though He were an old man, he was of an extraordinary vigor every way, and had every year a Child, had always a great appetite, and good digestion; and yet was not fat."

White Pyment

Ah-ha! This is NOT Sir Digby's doing! This is Tim's recipe. Enjoy.

Ingredients:

17 lbs honey (1.5 gallon)
48oz white grape juice concentrate
Yeast
4 gallons water
Yeast

Instructions:

Boil your honey and water as you would for basic mead, skimming it until it's clean. Remove from heat.

Add the concentrated grape juice.

Let cool.

Add your yeast and put the mixture into a fermentation vessel as you would for your basic mead, putting on your stopper and allowing it to ferment. After a month rack into a secondary fermentation container.

After 2 more months, rack again and taste. If it's too sweet let it ferment some more. If it's too dry, add a pound of honey.

After 2 more months, make sure the fermentation is stopped and bottle it.

Apple Pie Quick Mead

This is Tim's personal favorite and another of his own recipes.

Ingredients:

    11 pounds honey (1 gallon)

    2 gallons water

    2 gallons apple juice (preservative free)

    2 tablespoons cinnamon

    Yeast

Instructions:

Boil the apple juice and water together in your large pot or kettle. Once the juice is boiling add the honey, stirring constantly until everything is dissolved.

Continue to boil as long as a whitish scum is formed on the top of the must. Skim the scum that is forming off the top with a cheesecloth wrapped strainer.

When you've skimmed as much as you can, remove the must from heat and add cinnamon. Mix well.

While the mixture is cooling prepare your yeast as per package instructions.

Once the must is cooled to room temperature, transfer to the fermentation vessel. Add your yeast.

After 5 days rack and taste. If it is too sweet allow to continue fermenting.

Taste daily until the mixture is how you like it. If you think it's ready, kill the yeast or make sure the fermentation has stopped. Bottle.

METHAGLINS

T'ej—Honey Wine

T'ej is the traditional Ethiopian wine made from "honey raw with comb" cooked with gesho. Unlike other meads, this recipe does not call for yeast. Instead, the wild yeast that lives on the gesho is the fermentation agent.[34]

Gesho can be pretty hard to find unless you're in Ethiopia. You might try a resource like http://www.xtremebrewing.com to start off your hunt.

Ingredients:

---

[34] Brew using wild yeast with care. Medieval and ancient man seemed to get along fine using wild yeast as their fermenting agent, but it appears to be a dangerous practice in the here and now, especially in America where our natural yeasts are mean. Food poisoning and death are neither fun nor desirable.

16 fluid ounces honey (1.5 lb)

48 ounces water

Gesho inchet (sticks) or gesho kitel (leaves)

A wide-mouthed glass jar that seals tightly

Instructions:

Mix the honey and water in a large jar. Stir with a spoon until the honey is completely dissolved into the water. This will make the mixture foamy, but what's a little (or a lot of) foam. Seal and let sit for 24 hours.

Remove the scum from the top of your mixture and add your gesho inchet. How much you add will determine the taste of your t'ej. Ideally you would just cover the top of your liquid with the sticks and have some floating in the jar.

If you are using gesho kitel, use about 2 to 3 tablespoons per gallon of liquid.

Stir. If you're using kitel, stir until the leaves begin to soak up the liquid. Seal the jar and set aside for one week.

At the end of your first week, open the jar and stir the mixture. By now you may see white foam forming around the gesho. This is signs of the fermentation process. Unlike with mead, t'ej needs to be kept in as warm an environment through this as possible. Find a dry warm room or place it in your windowsill on a sunny day.

Seal the jar and put it aside for another week. At the end of that week, remove your gesho inchet with a pair of sterilized tongs. Get the mead as clean as you can, leaving no gesho in the fluid.

If you are using kitel, you will need to strain the liquid using cheesecloth as you would straining any other mead. You may have to strain your t'ej several times.

A proper t'ej has no gesho residue in it, so you may end up spending a lot of time cleaning the brew. Another point to make is you can stir your t'ej more frequently than once a week. Ethiopians say, "The t'ej likes to be stirred." Perhaps you should listen to what the masters say.

Return your spotless t'ej to the jar and seal for another two weeks. During these two weeks, stir your t'ej ever so many days.

At the end of these two weeks, strain your t'ej a final time. Now it is ready to chill and drink. Or bottle it. Keep it in a cool place like your refrigerator.

It is said t'ej can be stored up to 20 years.

METHELIN, OR HONEY WINE.

Adapted from the *White House Cookbook*: Just because this book isn't from the European Middle Ages doesn't mean it should be discounted for the facts it contains within. (Although some of Sir Digby's comrades would have been very unhappy to know that a woman wrote it as they believed a woman could not write a cookbook.)

The White House Cookbook is considered one of America's most enduring cookbooks, having been reprinted multiple times, sometimes under different names. Check out this methaglin recipe and see how very little things changed from one era to the next.

Once again, the language has been modernized. Purists are invited to find the original book, which is open domain and can be found in such places as Project Gutenburg, to enjoy this recipe and the others it has preserved.

Ingredients:

- 12 gallons spring water
- 33 lbs honey (3 gallons)
- 1 egg
- 2 ounces white Jamaica ginger, bruised
- 1 ounce clove
- 1 ounce mace
- 1.5 ounces cinnamon
- Yeast

Instructions:

To prepare, bruise and place your herbs together into a muslin bag. Tie securely.

Now strain your honey into your pot, and then add the water. Put the egg, unbroken, into the mixture. Put it on the heat and allow the mixture to boil.

When the egg floats at the top of the liquor, it is ready. Strain the mixture and pour it into a cask or other cooling vessel.

Place the muslin bag into the mixture. Add your yeast.

Now stopper your vessel and allow to ferment for six weeks.

Good mead

This recipe was adapted from an English translation of *Daz Bouch Von Guoter Spise*, which is a 14th century text. For this recipe, we put the German text at the end. If you speak Medieval German, it should be a treat!

Ingredients:

    2 gallons water
    11lbs honey (1 gallon)
    4 oz hops
    2 oz sage
    Yeast

Instructions:

Mix honey and water, put on heat and allow to boil until the scum stops rising, skimming it off as it does.

Allow to cool.

In a separate pan, boil the hops and sage together in1 cup of water. Add this to your must. Mix well.

Take off the heat and allow to cool to room temperature. Transfer to your fermentation vessel and add yeast as per package instructions. Stopper.

Allow to ferment for 3 nights and 3 days.

Rack to a new vessel and allow to ferment another 8 days.

Rack a third time and allow to sit for another 8 days.

Rack a final time, making sure the fermentation is done. If the fermentation is done, bottle.

Drink before 8 weeks.

Der guten mete machen wil, der werme reinen brunnen, daz er die hant dor inne liden künne. und neme zwei maz wazzers und eine honiges. daz rüere man mit eime stecken, und laz ez ein wile hangen. und sihe ez denne durch ein rein tuch oder durch ein harsip in ein rein vaz. und siede denne die selben wirtz gein eime acker lane hin und wider und schume die wirtz mit einer vensterehten schüzzeln. da der schume inne blibe und niht die wirtz. dor noch giuz den mete in ein rein vaz und bedecke in, daz der bra-

dem niht uz müge, als lange daz man die hant dor inne geliden müge. So nim denne ein halp mezzigen hafen und tu in halp vol hopphen und ein hant vol salbey und siede daz mit der wirtz gein einer halben mile. und giuz ez denne in die wirtz, und nim frischer hoven ein halp nözzeln und giuz ez dor in. und giuz ez under ein ander daz ez geschende werde. so decke zu, daz der bradem iht uz müge einen tae und eine naht. So seige denne den mete durch ein reyn tuch oder durch ein harsip. und vazze in in ein reyn vaz und lazze in iern drie tac und drie naht und fülle in alle abende, dar nach lazze man in aber abe und hüete daz iht hefen dor in kumme und laz in aht tage ligen daz er valle. und fülle in alle abende. dar nach loz in abe in ein gehertztez vas und laz in ligen aht tage vol und trinke in denne erst sechs wucher oder ehte. so ist er allerbeste.

Roses for My Love

Another recipe courtesy of the Nagger's father, adapted with a tad bit of research.

Ingredients:

    11 lbs honey (1 gallon)
    2-3 quarts fresh rose petals
    Ice cubes or crushed ice
    Water to make rose water
    Yeast
    A pot with a rounded lid

Instructions:

First make some rose water by taking a large pot, placing a fireplace brick in the middle with a bowl on top of the brick. Put your rose petals into the pot (around the brick) with just enough water to stand about 1 to 2 inches above the roses.

Put on heat and bring the water to a roiling boil. Lower the heat to put the mixture to a slow simmer.

When the mixture begins to boil again, put the lid on the pot, upside down (so it bows in towards the pot not away) and put your bag of ice in the top of the lid.

As the steam rises, it will condense on the lid (due to the ice) and run down to drip into the bowl in the middle. Ever so often, lift the lid and take out a couple of tablespoons of the rose water. Keep doing so until you have about a quart of water and it tastes and smells strongly of roses.

OR...you can just go buy some rose water and skip to the mead part.

Now, make your basic mead using the instructions from this book. Use the rose water for your must water, adding fresh water if you don't have enough for the recipe.

Heat the rose water and honey until they are blended. Do not boil.

Allow to cool and transfer to your fermentation vessel as you would for basic mead.

Add your yeast.

Allow to ferment with a stopper and airlock.

Taste your brew every two weeks. Rack if you feel

it is necessary. Once satisfied with taste, stop fermentation if necessary and bottle.

> Nagger's Note: you can also add rose petals to your must during the fermentation process for that extra rose flavor.

Rosemary Ginger Mead

This is a popular mead with variations found everywhere. This particular variation is courtesy of Sir Digby.

Ingredients:

3 lbs honey (1 quart)

1.5 gallon water

2 tablespoons of rosemary

1 tablespoon ginger

Instructions:

Add your honey and water together, boil, skim and basically do as you would basic mead. Remove from heat.

In a separate pan, boil the ginger and rosemary in a cup of water for 30 minutes. Mix your spice liquid to the must and allow the must to cool.

Once cool, move to your fermentation chamber and add yeast as you would for basic mead. Stopper with an airlock and allow to ferment until desired alcohol content and taste is attained.

Stop fermentation and bottle.

"Take to six quarts of water, a quart of the best honey, and put it on the fire, and stir it, till the honey is melted: and boil it well as long as any scum riseth : and now and then put in a little cold water, for this will make the scum rise: keep your kettle up as full as you did put it on; when it is boiled enough, about half an hour before you take it off, then take a quantity of Ginger sliced and well scraped first, and a good quantity of Rosemary, and boil both together. Of the Rosemary and Ginger you may put in more or less, for to please your taste: And when you take it off the fire, strain it into your vessel, either a well seasoned-tub, or a great cream pot, and the next morning when it is cold, pour off softly the top from the settlings into another vessel; and then put some little quantity of the best Ale-barm to it and cover it with a thin cloth over it, if it be in summer, but in the winter it will be longer a ripening, and therefore must be the warmer covered in a close place, and when you go to bottle it, take with a feather all the barm off, and put it into your bottles, and stop it up close. In ten days you may drink it.

If you think six quarts of water be too much, and would have it stronger, then put in a greater quantity of honey."

Trojniak

This is one of the traditional Polish meads. Some Polish claim that their mead stems back hundreds of years before the Age of the Vikings—and this might be true. If the Vikings plundered English women and Russian booty, why wouldn't they plunder Polish mead? Still, the Polish meads have a very distinct flavor and seem to be in a class all of themselves. Even Polish web pages have a completely different take on mead creation than their more English/American counterparts. "Trojniak" means "triple", making reference to the water to honey ratio.

Ingredients:

    22 lbs honey (2 gallons)

    3 gallons water

    10 teaspoons citric acid

    2 teaspoons tartaric acid

    1.5 teaspoons tannin

4 teaspoons yeast nutrient

2 oz hops

1 teaspoon ginger

1/2 cinnamon stick

Pinch nutmeg

6 cloves

2 pepper corns

Lemon peel

Orange peel

Champagne, sherry or madiera yeast

Instructions:

To prepare, tie your hops, spices and a stone or something to give it weight into a muslin bag.

Boil water; add honey, lemon and orange peels. Add your muslin bag, making sure it sinks to the bottom.

Boil for about 30 more minutes. Skim until clear.

Remove from heat, allow to cool.

Place liquid in fermentation vessel, add rehydrated yeast. Allow to ferment.

When it's done fermenting, skim it again and rack

to secondary fermenter. You may have to rack the mead several times.

This is the part where you need a lot of patience. Allow to ferment for two to three years. When you think the mead is ready, the sugar reading should be zero or less upon completion of fermentation.

Bottle and age at least one to two more years. Your minimum aging time total should be four years.

SACK MEADS

STRONG MEAD

Another old recipe from *The Closet of Sir Kenelm Digby.* Need we say more?

Ingredients:

11 lbs honey (1 gallon)

4 gallons of water

3 (or more) eggs

Yeast

Instructions:

To prepare, separate the yolks and whites from 2 of your eggs and beat the whites slightly.

Mix your honey and water together, boil until no

more scum rises, and skim clean the way you would for basic mead. HOWEVER, when the scum begins to stop rising, add in the beaten whites to help draw the last of the scum out.

Remove from heat and sink a whole (unboiled) egg into the must. If the egg floats to the surface with part of it above water, the must is ready. If the egg sinks, add more honey.

Remember if you do this test multiple times use a fresh egg each time. The liquid will boil the egg.

Once you are satisfied with how the egg floats, allow the must to cool to room temperature.

While waiting for the must to cool, you may finish boiling your test eggs in a separate pot of water and eat them if you're hungry.

Transfer the must to your fermentation vessel and add yeast, stopper and allow to ferment for three weeks.

After 3 weeks rack the mead to a second vessel and give it a taste test. If you are satisified with it, stop the fermentation and bottle. Otherwise let it ferment a little longer or until the fermentation stops naturally.

Then bottle.

Hide it away for a while. The longer you hide your mead away the better it will taste.

"Take one Measure of honey, and dissolve it in four of water, beating it long up and down with clean Woodden ladels. The next day boil it gently, scumming it all the while till no more scum riseth; and if you will clarifie the Liquor with a few beaten whites of Eggs, it will be the clearer. The rule of it's being boiled enough is, when it yieldeth no more scum, and beareth an Egge, so that the breadth of a groat is out of the water. Then pour it out of the Kettle into woodden vessels, and let it remain there till it be almost cold. Then Tun it into a vessel, where Sack hath been."

BOUCHETS

Also known as burnt mead, this is a drink *Le Menagier de Paris* contains under the section entitled BEVERAGES FOR INVALIDS. Finding information about this mead and the original recipes is difficult; the Nagger suspects that if it weren't for *Le Menagier* the art of making it would have been lost. Some say this has a caramel like flavor and smells like burning marshmallows while cooking.

We've adapted the bouchet mead into two recipes, drawing on *Le Menagier* for inspiration.

Spicy Bouchet

Ingredients:

18 lbs honey (1.5 gallon

3.5 gallons water

Yeast

1 ounce ginger

1 ounce long pepper

1 ounce grains of Paradise

1/2 ounce clove

Cauldron

Fire!

Instructions:

To prepare, place your herbs into a muslin bag. Tie securely.

You don't have to make this in a cauldron over an open fire, but the old recipe calls for fire and a cauldron. You can also make this in your brewing pot.

Put your honey into the cauldron and measure the liquid depth with a stick or ruler. Mark your measurement. You will need that later.

Put the cauldron over the fire and bring to a boil, stirring constantly. Do this for about two hours. While it's boiling it will grow in volume, getting to about double or triple its size. It will also put out little bubbles that will burst with smoke and begin to darken. Don't worry; just keep stirring to keep the honey from sticking to the bottom or scalding.

When the honey is dark (some say almost black), add 1/2 gallon of boiling water SLOWLY. Boil and stir until the liquid is back down to your original depth measurement.

Take the mixture off of the fire and put into cooling vessel. Add 2 more gallons of cool water. When it is room temperature, strain it through a cheesecloth into your fermentation vessel and add 5 gallons of water. Mix. Add your yeast. Add your muslin cloth of herbs, stopper and allow to ferment to taste.

> ***Nagger's Note:*** The original recipe in *Le Menagier* states to test the bouchet after two to three days to see if the mead smells spicy and is strong enough. If it is, you can remove the bag and squeeze it for reuse.

Four Year Bouchet

This recipe requires a great deal of patience. You can reduce the measurements to make a smaller batch to hide away in your closet for that special, distant occasion.[35]

Ingredients:

    1 lb honey

    3 lb water

    4.5 oz powdered cinnamon

    1.5 cloves

    1 of grains, beaten

Instructions:

Combine your water and honey together in a pot. You can do this all at once or cut the ingredients to

---

[35] La Menagerie says of this mead, "Note that the scum which is removed, for each pot of it take twelve pots of water, and boil together, and this will make a nice bouchet for the servants." Nice of those old rich folks to think of the people who kept their houses in order.

thirds to make three batches. With your stick/ruler, measure the liquid depth. Boil, skimming to keep it clean. Do this until the mixture reduces to a tenth.

If you chose to split your ingredients, put your must into a vessel and set aside. Make your next batch. Do this until you are out of ingredients or have enough must.

After about six weeks rack the bouchet into a new vessel.

Put your cinnamon, cloves and grains into a muslin bag and hang it by a cord or string into the mead from the vessel stopper.

Allow to stand four years.

> ***Nagger's Note***: You can also add spices if you desire to alter the taste (experiment and remember that you always get to drink the "failed" experiments).

**The berries of the grape with Furies swell
But in the honey comb the Graces dwell.**

THE MAKING OF TISWIN

This is a a fermented beverage made by Indians[36] of the southwestern U.S. It is not a mead, but we included it here for you Vikings to keep your Scraelings happy and out of your brew!

Get a lot of corn on the cob, shuck and shell it, and then place the corn in a container of water until it is soaked.

Spread your corn on a blanket—and let it sprout a little.

When it's sprouted, put it in the hot direct sun and let it dry up.

Grind your dried sprouts into the meal they de-

---

[36] Native Americans, whatever. The nagger is an American Indian and is among the large population of Indians who still use the word Indian.

serve to be.

Heat a pot of water and add your ground meal into it. When the water is about halfway boiled away, fill the pot back up.

Strain the water into a fermentation vessel and let it cool. Stopper it as you would your basic mead and let it ferment.

Don't drink until it stops bubbling.

Oh, the Beer Has Gone Flat? Make Mead!

In the old days, food was a terrible thing to waste. So was beer. So what did you do when your beer went bad? Here's an old answer from *The London and Country Brewer* included for your amusement.

"When strong Drink grows flat, by the loss of its Spirits, take four or five Gallons out of a Hogshead, and boil it with five Pound of Honey, skim it, and when cold, put it to the rest, and stop it up close: This will make it pleasant, quick and strong."

Happy Drinking!

A Verbose Bibliography and Resource List

"How to Use a Hydrometer" The Joy of Making Mead. May 21, 2012 .http://www.stormthecastle.com/mead/how-to-use-a-hydrometer.htm

"The Hydrometer & Its Uses" http://winemaking.jackkeller.net/advbasic.asp . May 21, 2012

Anonymous. The London and Country Brewer. London. Printed for Messeurs Fox, at the Half-Moon and Seven Stars, in Westminster-Hall. M.DCC.XXXVI. 1736

Arnald of Villanova . Von Bewahrung und Bereitung der Weine (The First Printed Book of Wine). Ulm: Johann Zainer the Younger, 1499. http://dfg-viewer.de/show/?set%5Bmets%5D=http%3A%2F%2Fdaten.digitale-sammlungen.de%2F%7Edb%2Fmets%2Fbsb0003510

3_mets.xml—free to read and explore if you read Ye Olde Germaine. Otherwise there are English translations to be found. Last accessed May 12, 2012.

Beran , Mark. The Past, Present and Future of Mead: Transcript from Mark Beran's presentation to the Boulder Revel, March 2006. http://medovina.com/history.htm

Bone, Katherine. Hidden Treasure-Historical Truth, Valkyria, Viking Heroine

Chaucer, Geoffrey. Oizumi, Aikio. Lexical Concordance to the Works of Geoffrey Chaucer. Olms, Georg Verlag AG, 2003. ISBN-13: 9783487119335—the only copy we could find of this was over $400 at Barnes and Noble. Thank goodness for Google books, which had the right page we needed available for preview online. http://books.google.com/books?id=1RyfoUvu-hMC&pg=PA735&lpg=PA735&dq=egremoyne&source=bl&ots=30saHa6h-N&sig=oy5g_32Kgk-rE-giAZqwGSKsMX2I&hl=en&sa=X&ei=ZEzPT6y_COa26QHfitzrDA&ved=0CD4Q6AEwAA#v=onepage&q=egremoyne&f=false

Ciesielski, Teofil. "Miodosytnictwo. Sztuka przerabiania miodu i owoców na napoje" ("Meadmaking. The art of converting honey and fruits into beverages"). 1925. We actually have this book in Polish and had to find translations for the good parts, so we can't give you much more about it than this.

Coppinger, Joseph. The American Practical Brewer and Tanner. NEW-YORK: PRINTED BY VAN WINKLE AND WILEY, No. 3 Wall Street. 1815.

Daz Buoch von Guoter Spise (1345) http://cs-people.bu.edu/akatlas/Buch/buch.html—
Sadly, the translation we found only gave permission to use the recipes within for private use. We have included this in the Bibliography for those that wish to find it and try the various recipes it contains for themselves. It has one mead recipe amongst a store of recipes for food.

Digy, Kenelm. The Closet of Sir Kenelm Digby Opened. 1669—This book is filled with recipes for wine and mead making. You could spend a lifetime experimenting with these recipes alone.

Eadie, Major J.I., D.S.O. An Amharic Reader. 1913.

Faith, Norah. Diet to Conceive a Boy. Ehow.com, April 13, 2012. http://www.ehow.com/way_5451961_diet-conceive-boy.html

Gillette, Mrs.F.L; Ziemann, Hugo. The Whitehouse Cookbook. The Whole Comprising A Comprehensive Cyclopedia Of Information For The Home. Chicago: R.S. Peale & Co.,

1887.

Huloet, Richard. Abecadarium Anglico Latinum. 1552, some place in England. We're not sure where.

K'Eogh, Joh. Botanalogia universalis Hibernica: or, a General Irish Herbal ...To which are added, two short treatises. One concerning the Chalybeat, waters, ...Another of the prophylactic, or, hygiastic part of medicine. George Harrison, 1735. http://books.google.com/books?id=Y3NbAAA AQAAJ&dq=marubium+album+herb&source =gbs_navlinks_s

Kurath, Hans. Middle English Dictionary, Volume 3. University of Michigan Press, Nov 15, 1966—128 pages.

Le Ménagier De Paris (circa. 1393)2nd. Edition.
http://gallica.bnf.fr/ark:/12148/bpt6k831118/f1
.image. Last accessed May 12, 2012. It should be noted that there are various translations and a scan of the original version to be found in various historical databases on the internet. The easiest for English readers to comprehend was translated by Janet Hinson; also it is known as "The Goodman of Paris" translated by Eileen Power.

Making Mead: the Art and the Science. National Honey Board, http://www.nhb.org

Martell, Hazel Mary. Food and Feasts with

the Vikings. New Discovery; 1st edition (August 1995)

Mayhew, A. L. (Anthony Lawson), b. 1842; Skeat, Walter W. (Walter William), 1835-1912 joint author. A concise dictionary of Middle English from A.D. 1150 to 1580. Oxford, The Clarendon press, 1888

Mead Hall. Wikipedia. April 13, 2012. http://en.wikipedia.org/wiki/Mead_hall

Pliny the Elder. The Natural History. John Bostock, M.D., F.R.S. H.T. Riley, Esq., B.A. London. Taylor and Francis, Red Lion Court, Fleet Street. 1855

Rigveda.
http://www.archive.org/stream/hymnsfromrigveda00macdiala/hymnsfromrigveda00macdiala_djvu.txt

Taliesin. The Book of Taliesin. Llyrgell Genedlaethol Cymru: The National Library of Wales. April 13, 2012. http://digidol.llgc.org.uk/METS/LLT00001/frames?div=0&subdiv=0&locale=en&mode=thumbnail

Tractatus de Magnetate et Operationibus Eius (13th century). Our version was an ebook version, but you can read it for yourself and view an image of the manuscript here:
http://www.uab.edu/reynolds/collect/manuscripts/tractatus/folios/49-tract20

Tyerman, Luke. The Life and Times of Rev. Samuel Wesley MA. London : Simpkin, Marshall & Co. 1819

THE PROMISED LIST OF OTHER MEAD TYPES

Acerglyn — Usually made from honey and maple syrup.

Balche — A native Mexican (Mayan) version of mead using the bark of the Balché tree (Lonchocarpus violaceus), This drink was used for religious ceremonies as it reportedly has halluciginogenic properties. We did try to find the recipe for larks, but we didn't get very far.

Black mead — A name sometimes given to the blend of honey and black currants.

Braggot — Yes, this is also a curse word.. but it's also a mead. Also called bracket or brackett.

Capsicumel — A mead flavored with chili peppers.

Chouchenn — A type of mead from Brittany.

Czwórniak— A Polish mead, made using three units of water for each unit of honey

Dandaghare — A mead from Nepal, combines honey with Himalayan mountain herbs and spices. This version is realtively new to the mead family, having it's start in 1972.

Dwójniak— A Polish mead, made using equal amounts of water and honey

Gverc or **Medovina** — Croatian mead.

Medica — Slovenian, Croatian, mead.

Medovina — Czech, Croatian, Serbian, Bulgarian, Bosnian and Slovak for mead. Give peace a chance.

Medovukha — Eastern Slavic variant.

Midus — Lithuanian for a melomel mead. This type of mead can be pretty strong, as much as 75 proof.

Morat — Mead made from honey and mulberries. Great for keeping your elves at bay.

Myod — Traditional Russian mead. In Russia, mead drink you.

Pitarrilla — Mayan drink made from wild honey, balché-tree bark and fresh water. This would be the receipe we couldn't include and don't recommend kids try at home.

Półtorak— A Polish great mead, made using two parts honey for each part water

Rhodomel — Made from honey, rose parts, and water. Makes you feel rosey.

Show mead — "Plain" mead, or your regular mead with no extras like fruit or flavorings.

Sima—A Finnish mead seasoned with lemon.

Tej—An Ethiopian mead.

Trójniak—A Polish mead made the opposite of the Poltorak, using two parts water for every one part honey.

White mead—Mead that is blanched (colored white) with herbs, fruit or, ew, egg whites.

HEARTBROKEN THE BOOK IS OVER?
CHECK OUT THESE OTHER TITLES!

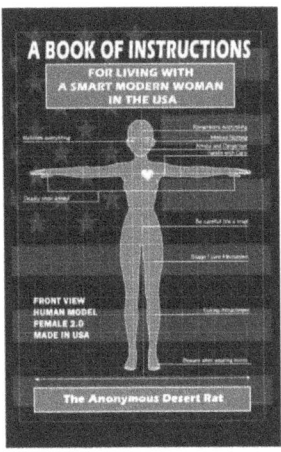

A Book of Instructions for Living With A Smart Modern Woman in the USA

A collection of warnings and anecdotes, by a long-term veteran of the marriage wars, illustrating the usual mistakes men make with women and how to avoid them. Be prepared for some unflattering R-rated advice!

There's Nothing Romantic About Washing the Dishes

Collection of short stories inspired by real life. Most represent an ethnic and mundane side from science fiction and fantasy writer, Katrina Joyner, people don't get to see often.

Ask about both titles at your favorite bookstore!

www.ingramcontent.com/pod-product-compliance
Lightning Source LLC
Chambersburg PA
CBHW070107120526
44588CB00032B/1374